THE COMPLETE JUICING RECIPE BOOK

101 Delicious Juicing Recipes That Help You Lose Weight Naturally Fast, Increase Energy and Feel Great

ERIK PELVIS

All rights reserved.

Disclaimer

The information contained in this Book is meant to serve as a comprehensive collection of strategies that the author of this Book has done research about. Summaries, strategies, tips, and tricks are only recommended by the author, and reading this Book will not guarantee that one's results will exactly mirror the author's results. The author of the Book has made all reasonable efforts to provide current and accurate information for the readers of the Book. The author and its associates will not be held liable for any unintentional error or omissions that may be found. The material in the Book may include information from third parties. Third-party materials comprise opinions expressed by their owners. As such, the author of the Book does not assume responsibility or liability for any third-party material or opinions. Whether because of the progression of the internet, or the unforeseen changes in company policy and editorial submission guidelines, what is stated as fact at the time of this writing may become outdated or inapplicable later.

The Book is copyright © 2023 with all rights reserved. It is illegal to redistribute, copy, or create derivative work from this Book in whole or in part. No parts of this report may be reproduced or retransmitted in any reproduced or retransmitted in any forms whatsoever without the writing expressed and signed permission from the author.

TABLE OF CONTENTS

TABLE OF CONTENTS **4**

INTRODUCTION **8**

JUICING FOR BEGINNERS **11**

    1. GREEN GODDESS JUICE 12
    2. GINGER ZINGER JUICE 14
    3. TROPI-KALE JUICE 16
    4. IMMUNE BOOSTER JUICE 18
    5. KALE KICKSTART JUICE 20
    6. CUCUMBER COOLER JUICE 22

JUICING FOR WEIGHT LOSS **24**

    7. POMEGRANATE JUICE 25
    8. WATERMELON JUICE 27
    9. GRAPEFRUIT JUICE 29
    10. CARROT JUICE 31
    11. CABBAGE JUICE 33
    12. CUCUMBER JUICE 35
    13. GREEN FRUITS AND VEGGIES JUICE BLEND 37
    14. ROOTS, LEAVES & FRUITS JUICE BLEND 40
    15. TROPICAL JUICE BLEND 42
    16. SWEET AND TANGY JUICE BLEND 44
    17. ORANGE DETOX JUICE BLEND 47
    18. REFRESHING JUICE BLEND 50
    19. LEMONADE BLITZ JUICE BLEND 53
    20. MORNING GLORY JUICE BLEND 56
    21. RED HOT JUICE BLEND 58
    22. CITRUS BLUEBERRY BLEND 61

- 23. WATERMELON ORANGE JUICE 62
- 24. BERRY BEET SPECIAL 64
- 25. SASSY SNACK 66
- 26. WEIGHT GOAL SHAKE 68
- 27. APPLE WATERMELON PUNCH 70
- 28. SWEET SHAKE 72
- 29. SUPER WEIGHT LOSS COCKTAIL 74
- 30. FEEL THE BURN FAT BURNER 75
- 31. CELLULITE BUSTER 78
- 32. GRAPEFRUIT WATERCRESS DELIGHT 79
- 33. TROPIC WEIGHT LOSS JUICE 81
- 34. RASPBERRY APPLE JUICE 83
- 35. JICAMA JUICE 85
- 36. ORANGE BONANZA 87
- 37. MINTY REFRESHER 88

JUICING FOR THE IMMUNE SYSTEM 89

- 38. CITRUS JUICES 90
- 39. TOMATO JUICE 92
- 40. ABC JUICE BLEND 94
- 41. SUNSHINE JUICE BLEND 97

JUICING FOR BETTER DIGESTION 98

- 42. LEMON JUICE 99
- 43. PRUNE JUICE 100
- 44. ANTIOXIDANT JUICE BLEND 102
- 45. GO GREEN JUICE BLEND 105

JUICING FOR HORMONAL REGULATION 107

- 46. CRUCIFEROUS VEGGIE 108
- 47. SOUR CHERRY JUICE 110
- 48. ORANGE-COLORED JUICE BLEND 113

JUICING FOR DETOXIFICATION 116

49. Apple Juice 117
50. Detoxifier Juice Blend.. 120
51. Ginger and Vegetable Zinger Juice Blend............. 123
52. The Detox Special 125
53. Borscht in a Glass 127
54. Glamorous Greens 129
55. Pomegranate Power 130
56. Boosting Body Cleanse 132
57. Iron Man.. 134
58. Total Body Detox 135
59. Carrot Cleanse... 137
60. Artichoke Cilantro Cocktail 139
61. C-Water Detox... 141
62. Papaya Strawberry Cleanse 143
63. Apple Cucumber Cocktail 145
64. Avocado Smoothie 147
65. Minty Melon Cleanser 149
66. Cranapple Magic... 151
67. Cabbage Kale Cleanse 153
68. Yamtastic.. 155
69. The Crucible 157
70. Cinnamon Cider.. 159
71. Root Vegetable Cleanse 161
72. Mango Tea 163
73. Drink Your Greens 165
74. The Detoxifier 167
75. The Vision... 169
76. Sweet Carrot 171

JUICING TO SLOW DOWN AGING 172

77. Red Grape Juice... 173
78. Cucumber Juice.. 175

- 79. YOUNG AND FRESH JUICE BLEND 177
- 80. YOUTHFUL PINK JUICE BLEND 179

JUICING FOR HEALTHY BODY 182

- 81. BLUEBERRY BLAST 183
- 82. ORANGE STRAWBERRY JUICE 185
- 83. ORANGE BANANA JUICE 187
- 84. SPICY CUCUMBER 189
- 85. BEAN MACHINE 190
- 86. POWER PUNCH 192
- 87. VEGETABLE SUPER JUICE 194
- 88. THE BEET MASTER 195
- 89. BLUEBERRY APPLE 197
- 90. THE ENERGIZER 199
- 91. LETTUCE PLAY 200
- 92. BEST OF BOTH WORLDS 201
- 93. SIMPLE PLEASURE 203
- 94. RED, WHITE, AND BLACK 204
- 95. PINEAPPLE CELERY COCKTAIL 205
- 96. CUCUMBER HONEYDEW PUNCH 207
- 97. MAGIC MEDICINE 209
- 98. NIGHT ON THE TOWN TONIC 211
- 99. CRANBERRY JUICE 214
- 100. POMEGRANATE JUICE 215

CONCLUSION 218

INTRODUCTION

Welcome to "The Complete Juicing Recipe Book," your ultimate guide to extracting the goodness and vitality of fresh fruits and vegetables through delicious and nutritious juices. In this comprehensive collection, we present you with an array of revitalizing juice recipes that will invigorate your body, delight your taste buds, and nourish your soul. Juicing has become a popular way to incorporate more vitamins, minerals, and antioxidants into our daily lives. With our busy schedules and fast-paced lifestyles, juicing offers a convenient and delicious solution to stay healthy and energized. From vibrant fruit blends to nutrient-packed vegetable concoctions, this cookbook showcases a diverse range of recipes that cater to every palate and dietary preference.

With each recipe carefully crafted to enhance flavors and balance nutritional benefits, The Complete Juicing Recipe Book ensures that every sip is a journey of wellness and pleasure. Whether you're a seasoned juicer or new to the world of extracting liquid goodness, we've got you covered with simple, step-by-step instructions that guarantee success in every glass.

Our commitment to providing the best juicing experience doesn't stop at the recipes. Each chapter is enriched with valuable tips, ingredient substitutions, and insights into the health benefits of the ingredients used. We believe that knowledge is key to making informed choices about the beverages we consume, and we're excited to share the secrets to a healthier and happier you.

As you dive into this juicing adventure, you'll discover how creativity and innovation can transform everyday fruits and vegetables into extraordinary elixirs. Whether you're seeking a refreshing pick-me-up, a natural immune booster, or a cleansing juice to detoxify your system, The Complete Juicing Recipe Book is your go-to source for all your juicing needs.

And let's not forget the joy of visual delight! Each recipe is accompanied by a colorful image that showcases the vibrant hues of the ingredients and the allure of the final creation. We believe that a feast for the eyes is just as important as a feast for the taste buds, and we've taken great care to ensure that the beauty of juicing shines through in every photograph.

So, grab your juicer, gather your favorite fruits and vegetables, and embark on a journey of health and wellness with "The Complete Juicing Recipe Book." Here's to delicious juices that awaken your senses, nourish your body, and bring a burst of vitality to your daily routine.

May your kitchen be filled with the aroma of freshly squeezed goodness and your life enriched with the goodness of nature's bounty. Happy juicing!

JUICING FOR BEGINNERS

1. Green Goddess Juice

Ingredients
- 3 stalks of celery
- 1/2 large cucumber, cut into quarters
- 1 medium green apple, cut into eighths
- 1 medium pear, cut into eighths

a) Juice all the ingredients following the instructions for normal juicing in your juicer manual.

b) Drink immediately, or let chill for an hour and then enjoy.

2. Ginger Zinger Juice

Ingredients

-
- 2 medium apples, cut into eighths
- 5 carrots (no need to peel)
- 1/2-inch fresh ginger
- 1/4 lemon

a) Juice all the ingredients following the instructions for normal juicing in your juicer manual.

b) Drink immediately, or let chill for an hour and then enjoy.

3. Tropi-Kale Juice

Ingredients

- 1/4 of a fresh pineapple, skin and core removed, and cut into 1" strips
- 4 kale leaves
- 1 ripe banana, peeled
- For Antioxidant Blast Juice:
- 2 medium beets, cut into quarters and the greens
- 1 cup blueberries
- 1 cup halved, hulled strawberries

c) Juice all the ingredients following the instructions for normal juicing in your juicer manual.

d) Drink immediately, or let chill for an hour and then enjoy.

4. Immune Booster Juice

Ingredients

-
- 2 oranges, quartered
- 1/4 lemon (remove peel for less bitterness)
- 1 medium apple, cut into eighths
- 1/2" fresh ginger

a) Juice all the ingredients following the instructions for normal juicing in your juicer manual.

b) Drink immediately, or let chill for an hour and then enjoy.

5. Kale Kickstart Juice

Ingredients

-
- 1 orange, quartered
- 1 cup halved and hulled strawberries
- 2 kale leaves
- 3 carrots
- 1 ripe banana

a) Juice all the ingredients following the instructions for normal juicing in your juicer manual.

b) Drink immediately, or let chill for an hour and then enjoy.

6. Cucumber Cooler Juice

Ingredients

-
  1/4 ripe cantaloupe, seeds removed, cut into chunks (no need to peel)
- 2 stalks celery
- 1/2 cucumber, cut into slices
- 1/4 lemon (remove peel to reduce bitterness)

a) Juice all the ingredients following the instructions for normal juicing in your juicer manual.

b) Drink immediately, or let chill for an hour and then enjoy.

JUICING FOR WEIGHT LOSS

7. Pomegranate Juice

Directions

a) Cut a fresh pomegranate in half, crosswise.

b) Lift the handle of your juicer and place one half of the pomegranate on it with the fleshy part facing down.

c) Press down using moderate pressure and watch as fresh juice flows out of the fruit. Continue pressing until you feel like you have extracted all the juice from the fruit.

d) Keep juicing pomegranate halves until you have enough juice for one glass.

e) If you want pure juice without seeds, you can pass it through a strainer first.

f) If the pomegranate fruit that you have juiced isn't sweet enough, you may add a natural sweetener to your juice. But if your main goal is to lose weight, then you may have to train yourself to enjoy fresh fruit juices without adding any sugar.

8. Watermelon Juice

a) Cut the watermelon in half then continue cutting the fruit into cubes.

b) Remove the seeds from the flesh. You may leave the white, tender seeds if

Directions

you don't mind a bit of texture in your juice.

c) Place the watermelon cubes in your juicer then press down to get fresh juice flowing. Continue juicing watermelon cubes until you have enough for one glass.

9. Grapefruit Juice

Directions

a) Rinse the grapefruit thoroughly using warm water.

b) Cut the grapefruit in half, crosswise.

c) Place one grapefruit half in your juicer with the fleshy side facing down.

d) Press down on your juicer until fresh, pink juice starts flowing.

e) Repeat these steps until you fill an entire glass with fresh juice.

f) By drinking grapefruit juice, you will boost your intake of vitamin C. This juice also contains dietary fiber, magnesium, and potassium.

g) Combine this with a healthy, balanced diet, and regular exercise, and you're sure to start shedding those stubborn excess pounds.

10.   Carrot Juice

Chop the carrots to make them easier to juice. But if you have a powerful juicer, you may skip this step.

Directions

a)

b) Place the carrot pieces in your juicer then press down until fresh juice starts flowing. Keep doing this until you have obtained one glass of fresh carrot juice.

c) Although it's best to enjoy carrot juice for breakfast, you can also drink it at any time.

d) Carrots contain antioxidants too, which can help boost your immune system. This is an important benefit if you're trying to lose weight.

11. Cabbage Juice

Directions

a) Choose a head of cabbage that is firm and has crisp leaves. This type of cabbage will produce more juice compared to heads of cabbage with limp, yellowing leaves.

b) Rinse the cabbage using cold running water.

c) Chop the cabbage head into blocks that will fit into the feeding chute of your juicer.

d) Place the blocks of cabbage into your juicer then press down until fresh juice starts flowing.

e) Keep adding blocks of cabbage until you have enough juice to fill one glass.

12. Cucumber Juice

Directions

a) Cut off the ends of the cucumber.

b) You may or may not peel it before juicing. Either way, make sure to rinse the cucumber first before you start slicing.

c) Cut the cucumber into pieces that will fit into the feeding chute of your juicer.

d) Add pieces of cucumber into your juicer and press down until fresh juice starts flowing.

13. Green Fruits and Veggies Juice Blend

Serving Size: 1 serving

Ingredients

- ½ lemon
- 1 cucumber
- 1 piece of ginger (fresh)
- 2 green apples
- 3 celery stalks (remove the leaves)
- a sprig of mint

Directions

a) Wash all of the fruits and veggies then use a paper towel to pat them dry.

b) Peel the ginger, apples, cucumber, and lemon.

c) Cut all of the ingredients into chunks that will fit into the feeding chute of your juicer.

d) Place the fruit and vegetable pieces in your juicer. Press down on the juicer until fresh juice starts flowing. Juicing the

ingredients will depend on the type of juicer that you own.
e) When you have enough juice to fill one glass, add the sprig of mint, and enjoy.

14. Roots, Leaves & Fruits Juice Blend

Serving Size: 1 serving

Ingredients

- ¼ pineapple
- ½ lemon
- 1 medium beet
- 1 orange
- 2 red cabbage leaves

- 3 medium carrots
- a handful of spinach

Directions:

a) Wash all of the fruits and veggies then use a paper towel to pat them dry.

b) Peel the pineapple, lemon, beet, carrots, and orange.

c) Cut all of the ingredients into chunks that will fit into the feeding chute of your juicer.

d) Place the fruit and vegetable pieces in your juicer. Press down on the juicer until fresh juice starts flowing. Juicing the ingredients will depend on the type of juicer that you own.

e) When you have enough juice to fill one glass, drink up!

15. Tropical Juice Blend

Serving Size: 1 serving

Ingredients

- ½ cup of pineapple chunks
- 1 large apple
- 2 large carrots
- 2 pieces of ginger (fresh)

Directions:

a) Wash all of the fruits and veggies then use a paper towel to pat them dry.

b) Peel the apple, carrots, and ginger.

c) Cut all of the ingredients (except the pineapple) into chunks that will fit into the feeding chute of your juicer.

d) Place the fruit and vegetable pieces in your juicer. Press down on the juicer until fresh juice starts flowing. Juicing the ingredients will depend on the type of juicer that you own.

e) When you have enough juice to fill one glass, you can enjoy your tropical juice blend.

16. Sweet and Tangy Juice Blend

Serving Size: 1 serving **Ingredients:**

- 1 cup of spinach
- 1 cucumber
- 1 lime
- 1 piece of ginger (fresh)
- 2 celery stalks (remove the leaves)
- 3 medium apples

Directions:

a) Wash all of the fruits and veggies then use a paper towel to pat them dry.

b) Peel the cucumber, lime, ginger, and apples.

c) Cut all of the ingredients into chunks that will fit into the feeding chute of your juicer.

d) Place the fruit and vegetable pieces in your juicer. Press down on the juicer until fresh juice starts flowing. Juicing the ingredients will depend on the type of juicer that you own.

e) When you have enough juice to fill one glass, enjoy this juice blend to calm your tummy, and make you feel better.

17. Orange Detox Juice Blend

Serving Size: 2 servings

Ingredients

- 1 orange
- 1 sweet potato (around 5 inches long, either cooked or uncooked)
- 2 medium apples
- 2 medium pears
- 3 celery stalks (remove the leaves)

Directions:

a) If you plan to cook the sweet potato, do this first.

b) Wash all of the fruits and veggies then use a paper towel to pat them dry.

c) Peel the orange, sweet potato, apples, and pears.

d) Cut all of the ingredients into chunks that will fit into the feeding chute of your juicer.

e) Place the fruit and vegetable pieces in your juicer. Press down on the juicer until fresh juice starts flowing. Juicing the ingredients will depend on the type of juicer that you own.

f) When you have enough juice to fill one glass, enjoy this sweet, and filling juice blend.

18. Refreshing Juice Blend

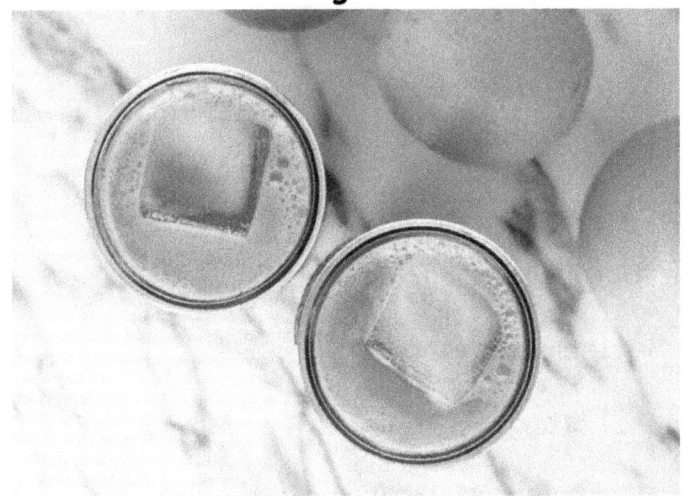

Serving Size: 1 serving

Ingredients

- ½ cucumber
- ½ piece of ginger (fresh)
- 1 lemon
- 1 orange
- 3 celery stalks (remove the leaves)
- 3 medium apples
- 4 kale leaves

Directions:

a) Wash all of the fruits and veggies then use a paper towel to pat them dry.

b) Peel the cucumber, ginger, lemon, orange, and apples.

c) Cut all of the ingredients into chunks that will fit into the feeding chute of your juicer.

d) Place the fruit and vegetable pieces in your juicer. Press down on the juicer until fresh juice starts flowing. Juicing the ingredients will depend on the type of juicer that you own.

e) When you have enough juice to fill one glass, enjoy this refreshingly healthy juice blend.

19.   Lemonade Blitz Juice Blend

Serving Size: 1 serving

Ingredients

- 1 cup of spinach
- ½ lime
- 1 lemon
- 1 piece of ginger (fresh)
- 2 celery stalks (remove the leaves)
- 2 green apples
- 4 kale leaves

Directions:

a) Wash all of the fruits and veggies then use a paper towel to pat them dry.

b) Peel the lime, lemon, ginger, and apples.

c) Cut all of the ingredients into chunks that will fit into the feeding chute of your juicer.

d) Place the fruit and vegetable pieces in your juicer. Press down on the juicer until fresh juice starts flowing. Juicing the ingredients will depend on the type of juicer that you own.

e) When you have enough juice to fill one glass, enjoy this tart, weight-loss promoting version of the classic lemonade drink.

20. Morning Glory Juice Blend

Serving Size: 1 serving

Ingredients

- 1 teaspoons spirulina (dried)
- 1 medium beetroot
- 2 medium carrots
- 2 oranges

Directions:

a) Wash all of the fruits and veggies then use a paper towel to pat them dry.

b) Peel the beetroot, carrots, and oranges.

c) Cut all of the ingredients into chunks that will fit into the feeding chute of your juicer.

d) Place the fruit and vegetable pieces in your juicer. Press down on the juicer until fresh juice starts flowing. Juicing the ingredients will depend on the type of juicer that you own.

e) When you have enough juice to fill one glass, add the spirulina, mix well, and enjoy!

21.   Red Hot Juice Blend

Serving Size: 1 serving

Ingredients

- 2 cups of spinach
- ½ lime
- 1 jalapeño
- 1 medium beetroot
- 1 piece of ginger (fresh)
- 2 celery stalks
- 5 large carrots

Directions:

a) Wash all of the fruits and veggies then use a paper towel to pat them dry.

b) Peel the lime, beetroot, ginger, and carrots.

c) If you want to reduce the spiciness, you may de-seed the jalapeño first.

d) Cut all of the ingredients (except the jalapeño) into chunks that will fit into the feeding chute of your juicer.

e) Place the fruit and vegetable pieces in your juicer. Press down on the juicer until fresh juice starts flowing. Juicing the ingredients will depend on the type of juicer that you own.

f) When you have enough juice to fill one glass, enjoy this unique juice blend with a kick.

22. Citrus Blueberry Blend

YIELDS 1 CUP

Ingredients

- 1 cup blueberries
- 2 oranges, peeled ● 1 pink grapefruit, peeled

Directions:

a) Process the fruits through the feed tube of an electronic juicer according to the manufacturer's directions in any order you wish.

b) Drink as soon as possible after preparation.

23. **Watermelon Orange Juice**

YIELDS 1 1/2 CUPS

Ingredients

- 2 cups watermelon chunks
- 1 large orange, peeled

Directions:

a) Process the fruits through an electronic juicer according to the manufacturer's directions.
b) Serve alone or over ice.

24. Berry Beet Special

YIELDS 1 CUP

Ingredients

- 1 cup blueberries
- 1/2 cup strawberries
- 1/2 medium beet
- 1 large leaf rainbow chard
- 1/2 cup spring water

Directions:

a) Process the berries through an electronic juicer according to the manufacturer's directions.
b) Add the beet and the chard.
c) Whisk the juice together with the water to blend and enjoy!

25. Sassy Snack

YIELDS 1 1/2 CUPS 1

Ingredients

- sweet potato, peeled
- 4 stalks celery, with leaves
- 1/2 cup spinach
- 1 zucchini
- 1 cucumber

Directions:

a) Cut the sweet potato into chunks and process through an electronic juicer according to the manufacturer's directions.
b) Add the celery and spinach.
c) Cut the zucchini into chunks and add it to the juicer, followed by the cucumber.
d) Whisk the juice thoroughly to combine and serve over ice as desired.

26.   Weight Goal Shake

YIELDS 2 1/2 CUPS (2 SERVINGS)

Ingredients

- 1 medium sugar beet, tops optional
- 5 carrots, trimmed
- 2 stalks celery, including leaves
- 1 cucumber, cut into chunks
- 1 grapefruit, peeled
- 1 kiwi
- plum, pitted
- pears, cored
- 2 apples, cored

Directions:

a) Process the beet and carrots through an electronic juicer according to the manufacturer's directions.
b) Add the celery and cucumber.
c) Add the grapefruit and kiwi, followed by the plum.
d) Add the pears and apples.
e) Whisk or shake the juice to combine the ingredients. Serve straight up or over ice.

27.   Apple Watermelon Punch

YIELDS 1 1/2 CUPS

Ingredients

- apples, cored
- cups watermelon, cut into chunks

Directions:

a) Process the apples through an electronic juicer according to the manufacturer's directions.
b) Add the watermelon.
c) Whisk the juice together to combine and serve immediately.

28.   Sweet Shake

YIELDS 1 CUP

Ingredients

- 1 banana, frozen or fresh
- 1 apple, cored
- 1 teaspoon pumpkin pie spice
- Bananas in the Blender

Directions:

a) Use a bullet-type juicer or blender to combine pulpy fruits such as bananas and avocados.
b) Combine all the ingredients in a blender and purée until smooth.
c) Serve immediately.

29. Super Weight Loss Cocktail

YIELDS 2 CUPS (2 SERVINGS)

Ingredients

- 2 stalks celery, including leaves
- 1/2 cucumber
- 1/4 head green cabbage
- 2 stalks bok choy
- 1/2 medium apple, cored
- 1/2 lemon, peeled
- 1 (1/2-inch) piece ginger

- 1/2 cup parsley
- 5 kale or collard leaves
- 1 cup spinach

Directions:

a) Process the celery and cucumber through an electronic juicer according to the manufacturer's directions.
b) Cut the cabbage into chunks and add to the juicer, followed by the bok choy, apple, and lemon.
c) Add the ginger and parsley.
d) Add the kale or collards, and the spinach.
e) Serve alone or over ice.

30. Feel the Burn Fat Burner

YIELDS 2 1/2 CUPS (2 SERVINGS)

Ingredients

- 2 large tomatoes, quartered
- stalks celery
- or 4 radishes, tailed and trimmed
- 1 sweet red bell pepper, seeded
- 1 yellow banana pepper, or 1 fresh jalapeño pepper, seeded
- 3 green onions
- 1/2 teaspoon cayenne pepper
- Generous dash of Tabasco sauce, or to taste

Directions:

a) Process the tomatoes and the celery through an electronic juicer according to the manufacturer's directions.
b) Add the radishes and peppers.
c) Add the green onions.
d) Add the cayenne and hot sauce.
e) Whisk the juice to combine and enjoy!

31.   Cellulite Buster

YIELDS 1 CUP

Ingredients

- 1 apple, cored
- grapefruit, peeled
- stalks celery, with leaves
- 1/2 cucumber
- 2 tablespoons fresh mint leaves

Directions:

a) Process the apple through an electronic juicer according to the manufacturer's directions.
b) Add the grapefruit sections, followed by the celery.
c) Add the cucumber and mint leaves.
d) Whisk or shake the juice to blend and enjoy!

32. Grapefruit Watercress Delight

- grapefruits, peeled
- 1/2 cup watercress or 4 sprigs of parsley

Directions:

a) Process the grapefruits through an electronic juicer according to the manufacturer's directions.
b) Add the watercress and parsley.
c) Serve the juice alone or over ice.

YIELDS 1 1/2 CUPS

Ingredients

33.   Tropic Weight Loss Juice

- 2 mangoes, seeded
- 1 apple, cored
- 1 grapefruit, peeled
- 1 (1/2-inch) piece of ginger

Directions:

a) Process the mangoes through an electronic juicer according to the manufacturer's directions.
b) Add the apple, followed by the grapefruit segments and the ginger.
c) Whisk or shake the juice to combine ingredients and serve.

YIELDS 1 1/2 CUPS

Ingredients
   34.   Raspberry Apple juice

- 2 cups raspberries
- 2 apples, cored
- 1 lime, peeled

Directions:

a) Process the berries through an electronic juicer according to the manufacturer's directions.
b) Add the apples, followed by the lime.
c) Whisk or shake the juice to combine ingredients and serve alone or over ice.

YIELDS 1 1/2 CUPS

Ingredients
   35.   Jicama Juice

YIELDS 1 CUP

Ingredients

- 1 whole jicama
- 2 cups spinach
- 1/2 medium beet
- 1/2 lemon, peeled
- 1 medium orange, peeled

Directions:

a) Process the jicama through an electronic juicer according to the manufacturer's directions.
b) Add the spinach.
c) Add the beet, followed by the lemon and orange segments.
d) Whisk or shake the juice to combine ingredients and serve over ice, if desired.

36.   Orange Bonanza

YIELDS 2 CUPS

Ingredients

- 2 small sugar beets, trimmed and tailed
- 2 large oranges, peeled
- 1/2 lemon, peeled
- large carrot, trimmed
- cups spinach
- 2 celery stalks with leaves
- 1 (1-inch) piece fresh ginger

Directions:

a) Process the beets through an electronic juicer according to the manufacturer's directions.
b) Add the orange segments, followed by the lemon.
c) Process the carrot, then add the spinach and celery. Add the ginger.
d) Whisk the juice to combine ingredients, serve immediately.

37.   Minty Refresher

YIELDS 1 CUP

Ingredients

- 1 apple, cored
- 5 sprigs of mint
- 1 lime, peeled

Directions:

a) Process the celery through an electronic juicer according to the manufacturer's directions.
b) Add the apple, followed by the mint and lime.
c) Serve alone or over ice.
d) Generous dash of hot sauce
e) Fresh herbs for garnish (optional)
f) Combine the ingredients in the work bowl of a food processor or blender until smooth.
g) Chill 1 hour or more and garnish with fresh herbs as desired.

JUICING FOR THE IMMUNE SYSTEM

38. Citrus Juices

Ingredients
- 3 tangerines or 2 small oranges - peeled
- 1 small lemon, peel cut away
- 1 small lime, peel cut away
- 1 inch of ginger peeled and thinly sliced
- 1/2 teaspoon dried turmeric, or 1/2-inch piece of peeled fresh turmeric
- Pinch of real sea salt
- Pinch of black pepper
- Honey, to taste (omit for Whole30)
- 1 1/2 cups water

Directions
a) Peel the tangerines or oranges, and cut the peel away from the lemon and lime. If you're using a high speed blender like a Blender all the fruit can be kept whole. Otherwise, you may want to cut it into smaller pieces.

b) Peel and thinly slice the ginger, and gather the other ingredients.

c) Add all ingredients to a blender. Blend on high until smooth and no pieces of fruit or ginger remain.

d) Serve immediately or move to the refrigerator to store until ready to enjoy. Shake before pouring!

39.   Tomato Juice

Ingredients
- 3 pounds very ripe garden tomatoes, cored, roughly chopped
- 1 1/4 cups chopped celery with leaves
- 1/3 cup chopped onion
- 2 Tablespoons sugar (to taste)
- 1 teaspoon salt
- Pinch black pepper
- A couple shakes of Tabasco sauce, about 6-8 drops (to taste)

Directions:
a) Put all ingredients into a large nonreactive pot (use stainless steel, not aluminum). Bring to a simmer and cook, uncovered, until mixture is completely soupy, about 25 minutes.
b) Force mixture through a sieve, chinoise, or food mill. Cool completely.
c) Store covered and chilled. Will last for about 1 week in the refrigerator.

40. ABC Juice Blend

Serving Size: 1 serving

Ingredients

- 1 green apple
- 1 lemon
- 1 piece of ginger (fresh)
- 2 beets
- 3 carrots

Directions:

a) Wash all of the fruits and veggies then use a paper towel to pat them dry.

b) Peel the green apple, lemon, ginger, beets, and carrots.

c) Cut all of the ingredients into chunks that will fit into the feeding chute of your juicer.

d) Place the fruit and vegetable pieces in your juicer. Press down on the juicer until fresh juice starts flowing. Juicing the

ingredients will depend on the type of juicer that you own.
e) When you have enough juice to fill one glass, enjoy this healthy juice blend that promotes immunity.

41. Sunshine Juice Blend

Serving Size: 1 serving

Ingredients

- 1 piece of ginger (fresh)
- 2 oranges
- 4 carrots

Directions:

a) Wash all of the fruits and veggies then use a paper towel to pat them dry.

b) Peel the ginger, oranges, and carrots.

c) Cut all of the ingredients into chunks that will fit into the feeding chute of your juicer.

d) Place the fruit and vegetable pieces in your juicer. Press down on the juicer until fresh juice starts flowing. Juicing the ingredients will depend on the type of juicer that you own.

e) When you have enough juice to fill one glass, enjoy this fresh, sunny, immunityboosting juice blend.

JUICING FOR BETTER DIGESTION

42. Lemon Juice

Servings: 6

Ingredients
- 3-4 Large Lemons to get 1 cup lemon juice
- 2 litres Water
- ¼ cup Sugar Optional or to taste
- 1 small lemon sliced Garnish (optional)

Directions:

a) Roll the lemons on the worktop in a circular motion or roll between your palms. This is so they are easy to juice.
b) Ingredients displayed.
c) Cut each lemons into 2 equal parts and juice.
d) cut lemons being juiced.
e) Pour the freshly squeezed lemon juice into a pitcher then add in 2 liters of cold water.
f) Add in the sliced lemons (Optional) and sugar if using.
g) juice and slices of lemon added in pitcher.
h) Stir well and put in the fridge to chill for at least 30 minutes or immediately serve on ice.
i) lemonade in cup and jug.

43. Prune Juice

Servings 2

Ingredients
- 1 + 1/4 cups water
- 5 prunes
- 2 teaspoons sugar
- 1 teaspoons lemon juice
- few ice cubes

Directions:
a) Take dried prunes. Add 1/4 cup water to it.
b) Keep covered and Set aside for 15-20 minutes.
c) To a blender add soaked prunes, 1 cup water then add sugar.
d) Blend it until smooth.
e) Extract the juice completely buy pressing with a spoon. Finally add lemon juice.
f) To the serving glass add few ice cubes, then pour the juice mix it and serve immediately.

44. Antioxidant Juice Blend

Serving Size: 1 serving

Ingredients

- 2 teaspoons apple cider vinegar (preferably organic with the 'Mother')
- ½ cup of parsley
- ½ beet
- 1 medium cucumber
- 1 small apple
- 1 small lemon
- 3 medium carrots
- 4 celery sticks
- ginger (fresh, you can add as much as you prefer) **Directions:**

a) Wash all of the fruits and veggies then use a paper towel to pat them dry.

b) Peel the beet, cucumber, apple, lemon, and carrots.

c) Cut all of the ingredients into chunks that will fit into the feeding chute of your juicer.

d) Place the fruit and vegetable pieces in your juicer. Press down on the juicer until fresh juice starts flowing. Juicing the ingredients will depend on the type of juicer that you own.

e) When you have enough juice to fill one glass, stir the apple cider vinegar in, and enjoy!

45.   Go Green Juice Blend

Serving Size: 1 serving

Ingredients

- 1 cucumber
- 1 green apple
- 1 lemon
- 5 kale leaves

Directions:

a) Wash all of the fruits and veggies then use a paper towel to pat them dry.

b) Peel the cucumber, apple, and lemon.

c) Cut all of the ingredients into chunks that will fit into the feeding chute of your juicer.

d) Place the fruit and vegetable pieces in your juicer. Press down on the juicer until fresh juice starts flowing. Juicing the ingredients will depend on the type of juicer that you own.

e) When you have enough juice to fill one glass, enjoy this fresh juice blend that will improve your digestion.

JUICING FOR HORMONAL REGULATION

46. Cruciferous Veggie

Ingredients

- 2 Tablespoons Mint Leaves
- 1 Cup Spinach
- 3 Stalks Celery
- ½ Cucumber
- 1 Cup Green Cabbage
- 1 Cup Broccoli (Stalks & Florets)
- ½ Red Apple
- 1 Small Lemon (3/4 of the peel removed)
- 1 Thumb-Sized Piece Fresh Ginger (peeled)

Directions:

a) Wash and chop all ingredients.
b) Run through juicer.

47.   Sour Cherry Juice

Serving Size: 1 serving

Ingredients

- ½ drop of basil essential oil
- 1 cup of kale leaves (chopped)
- 1 cup of pineapple (chopped)
- 1 lime
- 2 cucumbers
- 3 celery stalks

Directions:

a) Wash all of the fruits and veggies then use a paper towel to pat them dry.

b) Peel the lime and cucumber.

c) Cut all of the ingredients into chunks that will fit into the feeding chute of your juicer.

d) Place the fruit and vegetable pieces in your juicer. Press down on the juicer until fresh juice starts flowing. Juicing the

ingredients will depend on the type of juicer that you own.

e) When you have enough juice to fill one glass, add the basil essential oil to taste (and to add nutrition), and enjoy.

48.   Orange-Colored Juice Blend

Serving Size: 1 serving

Ingredients:

- 2 cups of greens like kale and spinach
- 1 beet
- 1 orange
- 1 small apple
- 3 carrots

Directions:

a) Wash all of the fruits and veggies then use a paper towel to pat them dry.

b) Peel the beet, orange, apple, and carrots.

c) Cut all of the ingredients into chunks that will fit into the feeding chute of your juicer.

d) Place the fruit and vegetable pieces in your juicer. Press down on the juicer until fresh juice starts flowing. Juicing the ingredients will depend on the type of juicer that you own.

e) When you have enough juice to fill one glass, enjoy this juice blend right away for the best results.

JUICING FOR DETOXIFICATION

49. Apple Juice

Ingredients:

- 18 Apples
- Cinnamon (optional)
- Sugar (optional)

Directions:

a) Start by washing and then coring the apple to remove seeds. Cut the apples into slices. There is no need to peel the apples.

b) Add the apples to the pot and add enough water to just cover them. Too much water and you'll have pretty diluted juice. This juice may come out a bit strong, but it's a lot easier to dilute the juice with extra water rather than trying to make the flavor stronger.

c) Slowly boil the apples for about 20-25 minutes or until the apples are quite soft. Place a coffee filter or piece of cheesecloth in your fine mesh strainer and place over a bowl.

d) Slowly ladle the hot juice/apple mixture into a fine mesh strainer and gently mash the apples. The juice will be filtered through the bottom into your bowl while the apple mush will be left behind. Place the mush in a separate bowl for later. Repeat this process until all of your juice is in the bowl.

e) Taste the juice after it's cooled for a bit. You can add additional sugar or cinnamon depending on your preferences. Again, if the flavor is too strong, you can add water a little bit at a time to weaken the flavor.

f) The apple mush you collected can easily be turned into apple sauce by puréeing and adding a smidgen of sugar and cinnamon to taste.

g) Keep in mind your homemade apple juice doesn't Berry Juice

50.   Detoxifier Juice Blend

Serving Size: 4 servings

Ingredients:

- ½ lemon
- 1 piece of ginger (fresh)
- 2 medium apples
- 3 medium beets
- 6 carrots

Directions:

a) Wash all of the fruits and veggies then use a paper towel to pat them dry.

b) Peel the lemon, ginger, apples, beets, and carrots.

c) Cut all of the ingredients into chunks that will fit into the feeding chute of your juicer.

d) Place the fruit and vegetable pieces in your juicer. Press down on the juicer until fresh juice starts flowing. Juicing the

ingredients will depend on the type of juicer that you own.
e) When you have enough juice to fill one glass, enjoy this juice blend, and store the rest in your refrigerator for up to a week.

51. Ginger and Vegetable Zinger Juice Blend

Serving Size: 1 serving **Ingredients:**

- ½ cup of parsley
- 2 cups of spinach
- ½ cucumber
- ½ lemon
- 1 green apple
- 2 celery stalks
- 2 pieces of ginger (fresh)

Directions:

a) Wash all of the fruits and veggies then use a paper towel to pat them dry.

b) Peel the cucumber, lemon, apple, and ginger.

c) Cut all of the ingredients into chunks that will fit into the feeding chute of your juicer.

d) Place the fruit and vegetable pieces in your juicer. Press down on the juicer until fresh juice starts flowing. Juicing the ingredients will depend on the type of juicer that you own.

e) When you have enough juice to fill one glass and enjoy this juice blend chilled for the best results.

52. The Detox Special

YIELDS 1 CUP

Ingredients:

- 3 medium sugar beets, including greens, trimmed
- 1 medium carrot, trimmed
- 1/2 pound black seedless grapes

Directions:

a) Cut the beets and greens into pieces.
b) Process the beets, greens, and carrot through your electronic juicer according to the manufacturer's directions.
c) Add the grapes.
d) Whisk the juice to combine the ingredients completely. Drink immediately.

53.   Borscht in a Glass

YIELDS 1 CUP

Ingredients:

- 2 small sugar beets, including greens
- 1 medium apple, cored
- 1 medium orange, peeled and segmented
- 3 green onions, including tops
- large cucumber
- 2 tablespoons fresh mint leaves

Directions:

a) Process the beets and greens through your electronic juicer according to the manufacturer's directions.
b) Add the apple, followed by the orange segments.
c) Add the onions and cucumber.
d) Add the mint leaves.
e) Mix the juice thoroughly to combine and serve over ice.

54. Glamorous Greens

YIELDS 2 CUPS

Ingredients:

- 1/2 bunch spinach, about 2 cups
- 1 cup watercress
- 1 cup arugula
- medium apple, cored
- 1/2 lemon, peeled

- stalks celery, with leaves
- 1/2-inch slice of fresh ginger

Directions:

a) Process the apple through an electronic juicer according to the manufacturer's directions.
b) Add the lemon and celery stalks.
c) Add the greens and ginger in any order.
d) Whisk the juice to combine and serve well-chilled or over ice.

55. Pomegranate Power

YIELDS 1 CUP

Ingredients:

- 4 pomegranates, peeled
- 1/2 lemon, peeled 2 tablespoons raw honey **Directions:**

a) Process the peeled pomegranates through an electronic juicer according to the manufacturer's directions.
b) Add the lemon.
c) Add the honey to the resulting juice.
d) Whisk the juice until the honey is completely dissolved and enjoy!

56. Boosting Body Cleanse

INGREDIENTS | YIELDS 1 CUP

Ingredients:

- 1 cup broccoli florets
- 3 medium carrots, trimmed
- 1 medium apple, such as Granny Smith, cored
- 1 celery stalk, including leaves
- 1/2 cup spinach leaves

Directions:

a) Process the broccoli, carrots, and apple through an electronic juicer according to the manufacturer's directions.
b) Add the celery stalk and spinach leaves.
c) Mix the juice thoroughly and drink as soon as possible after preparation for maximum effect.

57.   Iron Man

YIELDS 3 CUPS (2 SERVINGS)

Ingredients:

- 4 large oranges, peeled
- 4 medium lemons, peeled
- 1/4 cup raw honey, or to taste
- 4 cups red, black, or green seedless grapes

Directions:

a) Process the oranges and lemons in an electronic juicer according to the manufacturer's directions.
b) Add the honey, followed by the grapes.

c) Whisk the juice to combine completely and enjoy! If you prefer, add cold water to thin the juice slightly and lessen the intensity of the flavor.

58.   Total Body Detox

YIELDS 1 CUP **Ingredients:**

- 1 large tomato
- 2 stalks asparagus
- 1 medium cucumber
- 1/2 lemon, peeled

Directions:

a) Process the tomato and asparagus through your electronic juicer according to the manufacturer's directions.
b) Add the cucumber and lemon.
c) Mix the juice to combine and served chilled or over ice.

59.   Carrot Cleanse

- 1/2 pound carrots, trimmed
- 1 large apple, cored
- 1 lemon, peeled and seeded

Directions:

YIELDS 1 CUP **Ingredients:**

a) Process the carrots, one at a time, through your electronic juicer according to the manufacturer's directions.
b) Cut the apple into chunks and add.
c) Add the lemon.
d) Whisk the juice to combine and enjoy immediately.

60. Artichoke Cilantro Cocktail

YIELDS 1 CUP **Ingredients:**

- 4 Jerusalem artichokes
- 1 bunch fresh cilantro, about 1 cup
- 4 large radishes, tailed and trimmed
- 3 medium carrots, trimmed

Directions:

a) Process the Jerusalem artichokes, one at a time, through your electronic juicer according to the manufacturer's directions.
b) Roll the cilantro into a ball to compress and add.
c) Add the radishes and carrots.
d) Mix the juice thoroughly to combine and serve over ice as desired.

61. C-Water Detox

YIELDS 1 1/2 CUPS

Ingredients:

- 3 kiwi fruit
- 2 pink grapefruits, peeled and seeded
  - 4 ounces water

Directions:

a) Process the kiwi and the grapefruit through your electronic juicer according to the manufacturer's directions.
b) Add the water and mix thoroughly.
c) Drink as soon as possible after preparation as fresh vitamin C deteriorates quickly.

62. Papaya Strawberry Cleanse

YIELDS 1 1/4 CUPS

Ingredients:

- 2 papayas
- 1 cup strawberries, hull intact

Directions:

a) Process the papayas and strawberries through your electronic juicer according to the manufacturer's directions.
b) Stir together and enjoy!

63. Apple Cucumber Cocktail

YIELDS 1 CUP

Ingredients:

- 1 medium cucumber
- 1 medium apple, cored
- Water to make 1 cup juice

Directions:

a) Process the cucumber and the apple through your electronic juicer according to the manufacturer's directions.
b) Add the water to make 1 cup and mix thoroughly. Drink and enjoy!

64. Avocado Smoothie

YIELDS 1 1/2 CUPS

Ingredients:
- 2 leaves kale or Swiss chard, chopped
- 1/2 cup mango chunks
- 1/4 avocado
- 1/2 cup coconut water
- 1/2 cup ice

Directions:

a) Process the kale or Swiss chard and the mango chunks through an electronic juicer according to the manufacturer's directions.
b) Transfer the mixture to a blender and add the avocado, coconut water, and ice.
c) Blend until smooth.

65.   Minty Melon Cleanser

YIELDS 1 1/2 CUPS

Ingredients:

- 1/2 cantaloupe, peeled and seeded
- 1/4 cup fresh mint leaves
- 1/4 cup parsley
- 1 cup blueberries

Directions:

a) Cut the melon into chunks and process through an electronic juicer according to the manufacturer's directions.
b) Roll the mint and parsley into balls to compress and add to the juicer.
c) Add the blueberries.
d) Whisk the juice together to combine ingredients and enjoy!

66. Cranapple Magic

YIELDS 1 1/2 CUPS

Ingredients:

- 3/4 cup cranberries
- 3 medium carrots, trimmed
- 2 apples, cored

Directions:

a) Process the cranberries through an electronic juicer according to the manufacturer's directions.
b) Add the carrots and the apples.
c) Mix the juice thoroughly and serve.

67. Cabbage Kale Cleanse

YIELDS 1 1/2 CUPS **Ingredients:**

- 1 cup broccoli florets
- 1 small head red cabbage
- 3 large leaves kale or Swiss chard

Directions:

a) Process the broccoli through an electronic juicer according to the manufacturer's directions.
b) Cut the cabbage into chunks and add to the juicer.
c) Add the kale or chard.
d) Mix the juice thoroughly and serve alone or over ice.

68. Yamtastic

YIELDS 1 1/2 CUPS

Ingredients:

- 3 oranges, peeled
- 2 Anjou pears, cored
- 1 large yam, peeled

Directions:

a) Process the orange segments through an electronic juicer according to the manufacturer's directions.
b) Add the pears.
c) Cut the yam into pieces and add to the juicer. Serve over ice.

69.   The Crucible

YIELDS 1 1/2 CUPS

Ingredients:

- 1 stalk broccoli
- 1/4 head cabbage
- 1/4 head cauliflower
- kale leaves
- 1/2 lemon, peeled
- 2 apples, cored

Directions:

a) Process the broccoli segments through an electronic juicer according to the manufacturer's directions.
b) Add the cabbage, followed by the cauliflower.
c) Add the kale, followed by the lemon and the apples.
d) Whisk the juice together to combine and serve over ice.

70. Cinnamon Cider

- 2 apples, cored
- 8 stalks celery
- Dash of cinnamon

Directions:

YIELDS 1 1/2 CUPS

Ingredients:
a) Process the apples through an electronic juicer according to the manufacturer's directions.
b) Add the celery. Add the cinnamon to the resulting juice.
c) Whisk the juice together to combine and serve immediately.

71. Root Vegetable Cleanse

YIELDS 1 1/2 CUPS

Ingredients:

- 1/2 medium beet, tailed and trimmed
- 3 medium carrots, trimmed
- 2 apples, cored
- 1 medium sweet potato, cut into chunks
- 1/4 sweet Spanish or Vidalia onion, peeled

Directions:

a) Process the beet and carrots through an electronic juicer according to the manufacturer's directions.
b) Add the apples and sweet potato, followed by the onion.

c) Mix the juice thoroughly to combine ingredients and serve immediately.

72.   Mango Tea

YIELDS 2 CUPS

Ingredients:

- 1/2 mango, peeled and seeded
- 1 cup hot water
- 1 herbal tea bag

Directions:

a) Process the mango through an electronic juicer according to the manufacturer's directions.
b) Pour water over the tea bag and let steep for 2 minutes.
c) Add 1/4 cup mango juice to the tea and stir.

73.　Drink Your Greens

Ingredients:

-
    2 cups Baby Spinach Leaves
- 6 Celery
- 2 large Cucumber
- 1/2 Lemon
- 2 medium Apples
- 1-2-inch Ginger
- 1/4 - 1/2 cup Parsley Leaves

Directions

a) Wash, prep, and chop produce.
b) Add produce to juicer one at a time.
c) Serve cold over ice. May store in tightly sealed jars or glasses in the refrigerator for 7-10 days. Shake or stir well before drinking.

74. The Detoxifier

Ingredients:

-
  - 2-3 Beets
- 6 Carrots
- 2 medium Apples
- 1/2 Lemon
- 1-2-inch Ginger

Directions

a) Wash, prep, and chop produce.
b) Add produce to juicer one at a time.
c) Serve cold over ice. May store in tightly sealed jars or glasses in the refrigerator for 7-10 days. Shake or stir well before drinking.

75. The Vision

Ingredients:

-
- 8 large Carrots
- 2-3 Navel Oranges
- 1-2-inch Ginger
- 1-inch Turmeric (optional)

Directions

a) Wash, prep, and chop produce.
b) Add produce to juicer one at a time.
c) Serve cold over ice. May store in tightly sealed jars or glasses in the refrigerator for 7-10 days. Shake or stir well before drinking.

76. Sweet Carrot

- 10 large Carrots
- 2 medium Apples
- 1/4 cup Parsley (optional)

Ingredients:

-

Directions

a) Wash, prep, and chop produce.
b) Add produce to juicer one at a time.
c) Serve cold over ice. May store in tightly sealed jars or glasses in the refrigerator for 7-10 days. Shake or stir well before drinking.

JUICING TO SLOW DOWN AGING

77. Red Grape Juice

Servings: 6 servings

Ingredients
- 1-2 lbs. Red Grapes
- 2 cup Water
- $\frac{1}{4}$ cup Sugar

Directions:

a) Fill Blender with grapes.
b) Add water and sugar.
c) Strain pulp if desired.
d) Serve Chilled.

78. Cucumber Juice

Ingredients
- 6 cups water
- 2 English cucumbers
- 1 lemon juice and zest
- 2 tablespoons fresh mint

Directions:

a) Slice off the ends of the cucumbers and peel. Chop into a few larger pieces.
b) Place the cucumbers, water, lemon zest, lemon juice and mint in a food processor or in a blender. Blend the ingredients for 2-3 minutes until smooth.
c) Set a strainer over a larger bowl and pour the cucumber juice into the strainer. Use a spatula to move the juice through the strainer until no more juice strains out. Discard the solids.
d) Enjoy the cucumber juice immediately, or store in fridge for up to 24 hours.

79. Young and Fresh Juice Blend

Serving Size: 1 serving

Ingredients
- 2 cups of apples
- 2 cups of blueberries

Directions:

a) Wash all of the fruits then use a paper towel to pat them dry.

b) Peel the apple and chop it into chunks that will fit into the feeding chute of your juicer.

c) Place the fruits in your juicer. Press down on the juicer until fresh juice starts flowing. Juicing the ingredients will depend on the type of juicer that you own.

d) When you have enough juice to fill one glass, enjoy this anti-aging juice blend.

80. Youthful Pink Juice Blend

Serving Size: 1 serving

Ingredients

- ½ cup of strawberries
- 1 cup of blueberries
- 1 ½ cups of water
- 1 large kale leaf
- 1 small beet

Directions:

    a) Wash all of the fruits and veggies then use a paper towel to pat them dry.

    b) Peel the beet and remove the stem of the kale leaf.

    c) Cut all of the ingredients into chunks that will fit into the feeding chute of your juicer.

    d) Place the fruit and vegetable pieces in your juicer. Press down on the juicer until fresh juice starts flowing. Juicing the ingredients will depend on the type of juicer that you own.

e) When you have enough juice to fill one glass and enjoy this youthful juice blend that looks great and tastes even better.

JUICING FOR HEALTHY BODY

81.   Blueberry Blast

- 1 cup blueberries
- 2 large carrots, trimmed
- 1/2 cup fresh pineapple chunks

Directions:

a) Following the manufacturer's instructions, process the blueberries, carrots, and pineapple in any order you wish.
b) Stir or shake the juice to blend completely, adding ice as desired.
c) Drink as soon as possible after blending.

YIELDS 1 1/2 CUPS

Ingredients

82.   Orange Strawberry Juice

- 1 large orange, peeled
- 1 cup strawberries
- 1 banana, peeled

Directions:

a) Process the orange and the strawberries through an electronic juicer according to the manufacturer's directions.
b) Add the banana and transfer to a blender until the mixture is smooth. Serve immediately.

YIELDS 11/2 CUPS

Ingredients

    83.   Orange Banana Juice

- 1 small sweet potato, peeled
- 1 large carrot, trimmed
- 2 ripe pears, cored
- 3 medium oranges, peeled

Directions:

a) Process the carrot and sweet potato through your juicer according to manufacturer's directions.
b) Add the pears and orange segments and process.
c) Mix the juice thoroughly before serving.

YIELDS 1 1/2 CUPS

Ingredients
   84.   Spicy Cucumber

YIELDS 1 CUP **Ingredients**

- 1 cucumber
- 1 clove garlic, peeled
- 2 green onions, trimmed
- 1/2 jalapeño pepper
- 2 small key limes or Mexican limes

Directions:

a) Process the ingredients in any order through an electronic juicer according to the manufacturer's directions.
b) Stir to mix the juice and serve over ice.

85.   Bean Machine

YIELDS 1 CUP

Ingredients

- 2 cups fresh green beans
- 5 large leaves romaine lettuce
- 1 cucumber
- 1 lemon cut into quarters, peeled

Directions:

a) Process the beans through your electronic juicer according to the manufacturer's directions.
b) Add the lettuce, followed by the cucumber and the lemon.
c) Mix the juice thoroughly to combine the ingredients and serve alone or over ice.

86. Power Punch

YIELDS 1

Ingredients

- 1 medium yam, peeled
- 4 medium oranges, peeled
- 2 medium carrots, trimmed
- 1/2 cup fresh parsley
- 1/2 fresh pineapple, peeled and cut into chunks

Directions:

a) Cut the yam into pieces as required. Process through your electronic juicer according to the manufacturer's directions.
b) Add the orange segments, a few at a time.
c) Add the carrots and pineapple chunks.
d) Mix resulting juice thoroughly before serving.

87. Vegetable Super Juice

YIELDS 1 1/2 CUPS

Ingredients

- 1 whole cucumber
- 6 leaves romaine lettuce
- 4 stalks of celery, including leaves
- 2 cups fresh spinach

Directions:

a) Cut the cucumber into pieces and process through your juicer according to the manufacturer's directions.

b) Wrap the lettuce leaves around the celery stalks and add to the feeding tube.
c) Add the spinach, sprouts, and parsley in any order you desire.
d) Mix the juice thoroughly before serving.

88.   The Beet Master

YIELDS 1 CUP

Ingredients

- 2 medium beets
- 2 apples, cored
- 1 medium orange, peeled
- 2 stalks celery, with leaves

Directions:

a) Scrub and trim the beets. Cut into chunks.
b) Process beet chunks through the feed tube of an electronic juicer according to the manufacturer's directions.
c) Cut the apples into chunks and add to the juicer, along with the orange and the celery.
d) Mix the juice thoroughly and serve over ice.

89.   Blueberry Apple

YIELDS 1 CUP

Ingredients

- 2 cups fresh or frozen blueberries
- 1 apple, cored
- 1 wedge lemon or lime, peeled

Directions:

a) Process the berries through your electronic juicer according to the manufacturer's directions.
b) Add the apple, followed by the lemon or lime.
c) Stir or shake the juice thoroughly to combine the ingredients and serve.

90. The Energizer

YIELDS 2 CUPS

Ingredients

- 2 apples, cored
- 1/2 cucumber
- 1/4 bulb fennel
- 2 stalks celery, including leaves
- 1/2 lemon, peeled
- 1-piece ginger, about 1/4 inch
- 1/2 cup kale
- 1/2 cup spinach
- 6 leaves romaine lettuce

Directions:

a) Add the celery, followed by the lemon and the ginger.
b) Lightly tear the remaining greens into pieces and process.
c) Mix the juice thoroughly before serving. Serve over ice if desired.

91. Lettuce Play

YIELDS 1 1/2 CUPS

Ingredients

- 1/2 head romaine lettuce
- 1/2 head red leaf lettuce
- 2 sticks celery, with leaves

Directions:

a) Process the lettuces and celery through an electronic juicer according to the manufacturer's directions.
b) Serve the juice alone or over ice.

92.   Best of Both Worlds

YIELDS 1 1/2 CUPS

Ingredients

- 4–6 medium carrots, trimmed
- 1 medium sweet potato, peeled
- 1 red bell pepper, seeded
- 2 kiwis
- 1-inch piece ginger
- 1/2 lemon, peeled
- 2 stalks celery, with leaves

Directions:

a) Process the carrots through an electronic juicer according to the manufacturer's directions.
b) Add the sweet potato, followed by the pepper.
c) Add the kiwis and the ginger.
d) Add the lemon and the celery.
e) Whisk or shake the juice thoroughly to combine and serve alone or over ice.

93. Simple Pleasure

YIELDS 1 CUP

Ingredients

- 4 large carrots, trimmed
- 1 orange, peeled

Directions:

a) Process the carrots through an electronic juicer according to the manufacturer's directions.
b) Add the orange segments.
c) Whisk or shake the juice to combine, and serve.

94.   Red, White, and Black

YIELDS 1 1/2 CUPS

Ingredients

- 1 cup red grapes
- 1 cup white grapes
- 1/2 cup black currants

Directions:

a) Process the grapes through an electronic juicer according to the manufacturer's directions.
b) Add the currants.
c) Serve the juice alone or over ice.

95. Pineapple Celery Cocktail

YIELDS 1 CUP

Ingredients

- 3 (1-inch) slices fresh pineapple, peeled
- 3 stalks celery, with leaves

Directions:

a) Process the pineapple chunks and celery through your juicer.
b) Serve the juice immediately.

96. Cucumber Honeydew Punch

YIELDS 2 CUPS

Ingredients

- 1/2 cucumber
- 1/4 small honeydew melon
- 1 cup seedless green grapes
- 2 kiwi fruits, peeled
- 3/4 cup spinach
- 1 Sprig of mint
- 1 lemon, peeled

Directions:

a) Process the cucumber and melon through an electronic juicer according to the manufacturer's directions.
b) Add the grapes and the kiwis.
c) Add the spinach and the mint, followed by the lemon.
d) Mix the juice thoroughly to combine ingredients and serve immediately.

97. Magic Medicine

YIELDS 1 CUP

Ingredients

- 1 mango, peeled and cored
- 1/2 cup peaches
- 1/2 cup pineapple chunks
- 2 tablespoons raw honey
- 1 teaspoon fresh grated ginger
- 1 cup blueberries

Directions:

a) Process the mango through your electronic juicer according to the manufacturer's directions.
b) Add the peaches and pineapples chunks, a few at a time.
c) Mix the honey with the ginger and blueberries and add to the juicer.
d) Mix the juice thoroughly before serving.

98.   Night on the Town Tonic

INGREDIENTS | YIELDS 2 1/2 CUPS (2 SERVINGS)

Ingredients

- 1 small beet
- 6 medium carrots, trimmed
- 1 green pepper, seeded
- 1 red bell pepper, seeded
- 1/2 cup kale
- 2 cups baby spinach leaves
- 2 large tomatoes
- 1/4 head fresh cabbage
- 2 stalks celery
- 2 green onions, trimmed
- 1 small clove garlic, peeled
- 1 teaspoon salt • Hot pepper sauce, to taste

Directions:

a) Process the beet and the carrots through your electronic juicer according to the manufacturer's directions.
b) Add the peppers, followed by the kale and spinach.

c) Add the tomatoes, cabbage, and celery
d) Last, add the onions and garlic and salt.
e) Whisk the juice thoroughly to combine, season to taste with hot sauce, and serve over ice to increase hydration.

99.   Cranberry Juice

Ingredients
- 2 quarts water
- 8 cups fresh or frozen cranberries
- 1-1/2 cups sugar
- 1/2 cup lemon juice
- 1/2 cup orange juice

Directions
a) In a Dutch oven or large saucepan, bring water and cranberries to a boil. Reduce

heat; cover and simmer until berries begin to pop, 20 minutes.

b) Strain through a fine strainer, pressing mixture with a spoon; discard berries. Return cranberry juice to the pan. Stir in the sugar, lemon juice and orange juice. Bring to a boil; cook and stir until sugar is dissolved.

c) Remove from the heat. Cool. Transfer to a pitcher; cover and refrigerate until chilled.

100. Pomegranate Juice

Ingredients
- 5 to 6 large pomegranates

Directions:
a) Using a paring knife, remove the part of the pomegranate that looks like a crown. I like angling my paring knife downward and making a circle around the crown.
b) Score the pomegranate into sections. I find scoring the fruit 4 times is enough for me, but feel free to score it a few more times.
c) Break open the pomegranate into sections.
d) Fill a large bowl with cool water. Break apart the pomegranate underneath the water. It helps prevent pomegranate juice from squirting everywhere.
e) Drain the water from the pomegranate when you're done separating them from the rind.
f) Pour into a blender. Blend until all the arils have been crushed but most of the seeds are still intact. This usually takes no more than 15 to 20 seconds.

g) Pour the juice through a strainer. You'll notice that the juice passes through the strainer pretty slowly because the pulp is pretty thick. To speed up the process, use a rubber spatula to press the pulp against the strainer. The juice should drip through faster.

h) Pour juice into a glass to serve. 5 to 6 large pomegranates should yield about 4 cups of juice. Leftover juice can be refrigerated in a jar for 5 to 6 days.

CONCLUSION

There you have it!

Everything you need to know about juicing. By now, you are already armed with the information you need to start your own juicing journey safely and correctly. As promised at the beginning of the book, I shared with you everything I learned and discovered throughout my juicing journey. We started this eBook by defining what juicing is, answered the most important question related to juicing, discussed the benefits of juicing, and you even learned the most important things to keep in mind when you start juicing. The next chapter was all about finding the perfect juicer. Here, you learned all about the different types of juicers along with the whole process of how to find the best

www.ingramcontent.com/pod-product-compliance
Lightning Source LLC
Chambersburg PA
CBHW050347120526
44590CB00015B/1596